WILDLIFE SURVIVAL

Rhinos
in DANGER

by Helen Orme

Consultant: The International Rhino Foundation

BEARPORT
PUBLISHING

New York, New York

Credits

Corbis: 9, 14, 15, 18, 19, 22–23, 25, 27, 29, 30, 32. Oxford Scientific Photo Library: 25. Shutterstock: Cover, 4–5, 6, 8, 10–11, 12–13, 16–17, 20–21, 22–23, 26. Superstock: 6.
Every effort has been made to trace the copyright holders, and we apologize in advance for any unintentional omissions. We would be pleased to insert the appropriate acknowledgments in any subsequent edition of this publication.

Library of Congress Cataloging-in-Publication Data

Orme, Helen.
  Rhinos in danger / by Helen Orme.
      p. cm. — (Wildlife survival)
  Includes bibliographical references and index.
  ISBN-13: 978-1-59716-265-4 (library binding)
  ISBN-10: 1-59716-265-5 (library binding)
  ISBN-13: 978-1-59716-293-7 (pbk.)
  ISBN-10: 1-59716-293-0 (pbk.)
  1. Rhinoceros (Genus) — Juvenile literature. I. Title. II. Series.

  QL737.U63O76 2007   **3 0691 00165812 9**
  599.66'8—dc22

                          2006012273

For more information, write to Bearport Publishing Company, Inc., 101 Fifth Avenue, Suite 6R, New York, New York 10003. Printed in the United States of America.

10 9 8 7 6 5 4 3 2 1

The Wildlife Survival series was originally developed by ticktock Media Ltd.

Table of Contents

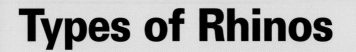

Types of Rhinos

The word *rhino* is short for rhinoceros, which means "nose horn." There are five different types of rhinos in the world. Two kinds of rhinos live on the grassy plains of southern Africa. The other kinds of rhinos live in the forests of India and in several countries in Southeast Asia.

All types of rhinos are endangered. Some of these animals are very close to disappearing completely.

A male African rhino

African Rhinos

The black rhino and the white rhino live in Africa. They don't look like their names, though. They are both the same color—gray!

African rhinos live on open plains called **savannahs**. They are plant-eaters and like grass and leaves from bushes that are close to the ground.

Africans refer to the white rhinos as "wide mouthed" rhinos. This name was given to the animals because they have larger mouths than black rhinos. When Europeans first visited Africa, they thought the local people were saying "white" not "wide." It was this mistake that led to the name white rhinos.

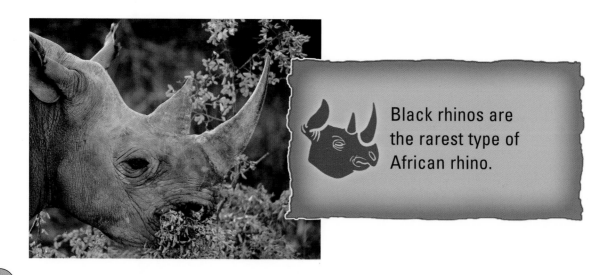

Black rhinos are the rarest type of African rhino.

An African white rhino

Asian Rhinos

Three types of rhinos live in Asia. Indian rhinos live in open places near rivers in the north of India and in Nepal. The Sumatran rhino lives in the forests of Borneo and Sumatra. This animal is sometimes called the "hairy rhinoceros" because it has a shaggy coat of hair. The Javan rhino is the rarest of all the rhinos. Only about 60 of them are left in the world. They live in Java and Vietnam.

The Indian rhino is also known as the "greater one-horned" rhino. It's the largest of the three types of Asian rhinos.

A hairy Sumatran rhino

9

Feeding

All rhinos are **herbivores**. However, different types of rhinos eat in different ways. White rhinos are grazers. They eat grass and other plants found on the ground. Browsers, such as the black rhino, eat leaves growing on bushes and trees.

Each type of eater has a differently shaped mouth. Grazers have wide mouths. Browsers have narrow mouths with pointed lips. The different shapes help the rhinos get the kind of food they need.

Rhinos spend most of their day looking for food and drinking at water holes.

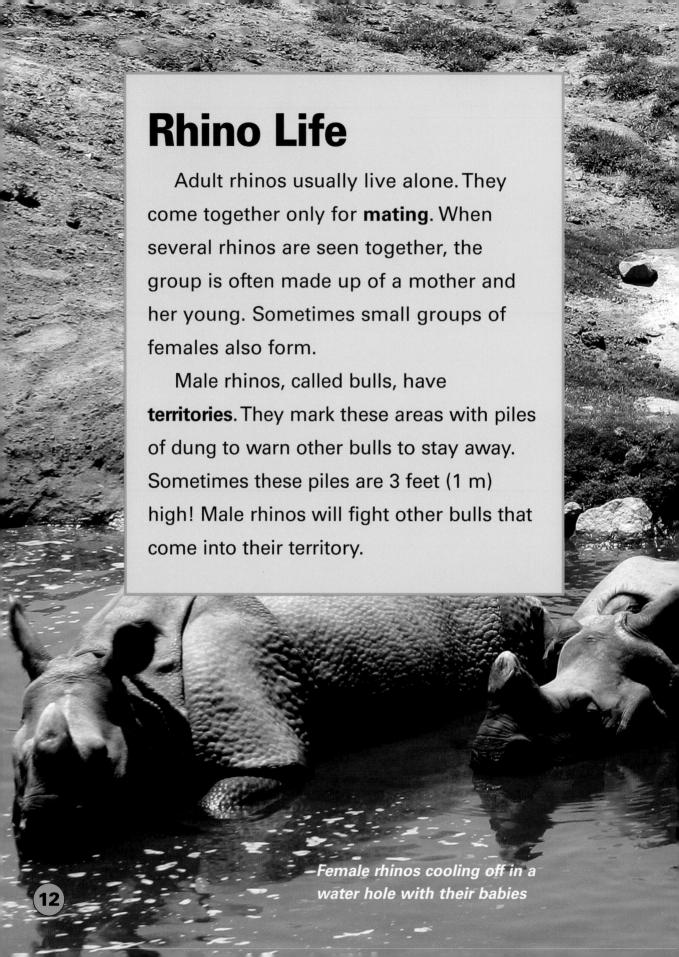

Rhino Life

Adult rhinos usually live alone. They come together only for **mating**. When several rhinos are seen together, the group is often made up of a mother and her young. Sometimes small groups of females also form.

Male rhinos, called bulls, have **territories**. They mark these areas with piles of dung to warn other bulls to stay away. Sometimes these piles are 3 feet (1 m) high! Male rhinos will fight other bulls that come into their territory.

Female rhinos cooling off in a water hole with their babies

Baby rhinos are called calves.

Charging Rhinos

Many people believe that rhinos are dangerous. They think these animals will charge for no reason. This belief is not true, however. If frightened by people or other animals, a rhino will run—but usually in the opposite direction. These fast runners move at speeds of up to 31 miles per hour (50 kph)!

White and Indian rhino calves usually run in front of their mothers. The babies of the black, Javan, and Sumatran rhinos run behind their mothers.

A white rhino with her calf running in front

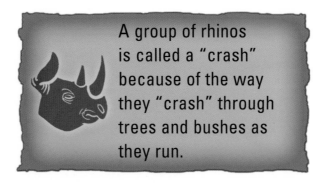

A group of rhinos is called a "crash" because of the way they "crash" through trees and bushes as they run.

Horns

Black, white, and Sumatran rhinos have two horns. Indian and Javan rhinos have only one horn.

Male rhinos use their horns when they're fighting to defend their territories. The front horn of a male white rhino can grow as long as 4.3 feet (1.3 m).

Some people believe that a rhino's horn can cure illnesses. They crush the horn into a powder to use in making medicines. Many rhinos have been killed for their horns. Today, **poaching** is the main reason these animals are endangered.

 Rhino horns can't actually cure people who are sick. The horns are made of keratin, the same material that human fingernails are made of.

Habitat Loss

Rhinos are animals that need lots of land. They roam over large areas to find enough food to eat. In Africa and Asia, however, more and more of their land is being taken away. The human **population** in the area where the rhinos live is growing. More food is needed for these people. So the rhinos' **habitat** is being turned into farms to grow food. To survive, most rhinos have to live in protected **wildlife reserves**.

The forests where the Sumatran rhinos live are being cut down by **loggers**. The wood is sold and the land is used for farms.

Rhinos in a wildlife reserve with a park ranger, who guards them

Climate Change

Another big problem for rhinos and other wild animals is the changing **climate**. These changes can cause **droughts**. If water holes dry up, rhinos will have to travel longer distances for a drink. They might not be able to find enough water to survive!

When there is less rain, some types of plants, such as grasses, begin to disappear. If there is no grass, some rhinos will starve.

Drought can also cause deserts to spread.

Saving the Rhino

People are trying very hard to protect rhinos. Zoos around the world have set up **breeding programs**. In Africa and Asia, wildlife reserves are meant to provide safe homes for the animals. However, poachers still get in sometimes and kill the rhinos.

One way to help rhinos is for **tourists** to visit the animals in their natural habitat. Wildlife tourism brings in money for the countries where rhinos live. This money makes protecting the rhinos important to local people.

Poachers kill rhinos for their skin as well. Some people believe that the skin can cure sickness. However, this is not true.

Where Do Rhinos Live?

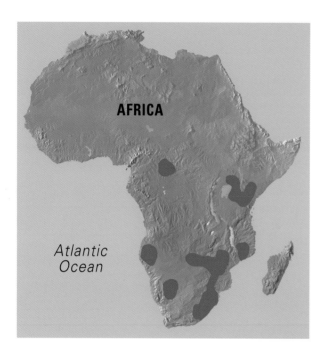

AFRICA

Atlantic Ocean

■ African rhinos live in grasslands in eastern and southern Africa. These areas are shown in red on the map.

■ Indian rhinos live in open areas in northern India and southern Nepal, shown in orange on the map.

■ Sumatran and Javan rhinos live in swamps and forests in Nepal, Malaysia, and Indonesia, shown in yellow on the map.

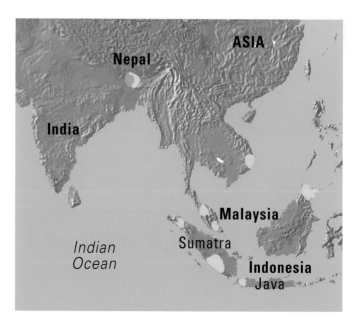

ASIA

Nepal

India

Malaysia

Sumatra

Indonesia

Java

Indian Ocean

More About Rhino Bodies

- White rhinos are the biggest of all the rhinos. After the elephant, they are the largest **mammals** that live on land.

- Both male and female rhinos have horns.

- A rhino's biggest muscles are in its neck. These muscles are needed to hold up the rhino's huge head.

- A rhino's skin looks tough, but it can be damaged by the sun and insect bites. Rhinos keep their skin covered in mud to protect themselves.

The Biggest

Length: 13 feet (4 m)
Height: up to 6 feet (1.8 m)
Weight: up to 5,071 pounds (2,300 kg)

The Smallest

Length: up to 10 feet (3 m)
Height: up to 5 feet (1.5 m)
Weight: up to 1,764 pounds (800 kg)

Rhino Calves

- Rhino mothers have their first babies when they are about 8 years old. After that, they can have calves every 2 to 4 years.

- Rhinos have only 1 baby at a time.

- Male rhinos don't help take care of the calves.

- Baby rhinos stay with their mothers for at least 2 years.

- If a **predator**, such as a crocodile or a lion, comes near, a mother rhino will protect her calf by standing over it.

More About Rhino Life

- Rhinos have poor eyesight. However, they have a very good sense of smell. Rhinos use smell to recognize one another, find food, and keep out of danger.

- Adult rhinos have no natural predators. In the wild, a rhino can live to be 40 years old.

- The rhino's best friend is the tick bird. This bird sits on the rhino and eats insects off its skin.

A rhino cooling off in the mud

Rhinos in Danger

- Animal experts believe that 200 years ago there were more than 1 million rhinos in the world. Now there are fewer than 19,000.

- Rhino horns are very valuable. They are often worth more than gold.

- There is some good news—the number of African rhinos is going up slightly.

How many rhinos?	
Type of Rhino	**Number Left Today**
White rhinos	12,000
Black rhinos	3,700
Indian rhinos	2,550
Sumatran rhinos	300
Javan rhinos	60

Conservation

- Wildlife reserves have been set up in Africa and India. Some reserves have strong fences to keep out poachers. However, even in the reserves, poaching still happens.

- One way to help humans and animals live together is to involve local people in wildlife tourism. Tourists need places to stay, guides, and food. When local people provide these things, they make money. It then becomes important to locals to keep the rhinos safe.

- In some reserves, groups of rhinos are watched over by guards with guns. At night, the rhinos are locked up and guarded. However, some poachers will kill the guards just to get at the rhinos.

- Some **conservationists** remove the horns from wild rhinos. This process doesn't hurt the rhino—it's sort of like cutting a person's fingernails. If the rhino's horn is gone, there is no reason for poachers to kill it.

How to Help

Conservation is everyone's job. Here are some ways to help rhinos:

- Learn more about rhinos. Then teach others at school about the importance of helping them.

- Help an organization, such as the African Wildlife Foundation (AWF) (www.awf.org). Groups such as this one raise money to pay for conservation work. To help the AWF or another conservation group, have a yard sale. Sell old clothes, toys, and books. Then donate the money that is made to the group.

- Ask your teacher if your class can adopt a rhino. (Don't worry, it won't live in your classroom.) Go to a reliable Web site, such as www.sheldrickwildlifetrust.org, to see how to adopt a rhino calf or a rhino family.

- Be a good conservationist. Visit www.worldwildlife.org/act/action.cfm for tips on how to help take care of the world.

Visit these Web sites for more information on rhinos and how to help them:

www.enchantedlearning.com/subjects/
mammals/rhino/Rhinoprintout.shtml

www.nationalgeographic.com/kids/
creature_feature/0205/rhinos2.html

www.rhinos-irf.org/savetherhinos/

www.worldwildlife.org/rhinos/

Glossary

breeding programs (BREED-ing PROH-gramz) plans that allow zoos to keep rare animals and help them breed by giving them mates; the zoos also help keep the babies healthy

climate (KLYE-mit) having to do with the weather in an area

conservationists (*kon*-sur-VAY-shuhn-ists) people who take care of the natural world; they try to stop others from hunting endangered animals and ask governments to pass laws to protect wild habitats

droughts (DROUTS) long periods of time without rain

habitat (HAB-uh-*tat*) a place in the wild where an animal or plant lives

herbivores (HUR-buh-vohrz) animals that eat only plants and no meat

loggers (LOG-urz) people who cut down trees to sell for wood

mammals (MAM-uhlz) warm-blooded animals that have hair and nurse their offspring

mating (MATE-ing) joining together to breed

poaching (POHCH-ing) hunting illegally on someone else's land in order to capture or kill an animal so that it can be sold for money

population (*pop*-yuh-LAY-shuhn) the total number of people who live in an area

predator (PRED-uh-tur) an animal that lives by killing and eating other animals

savannahs (suh-VAN-uhz) large, open areas of land in Africa where grass and bushes grow

territories (TER-uh-*tor*-eez) areas of land that belong to animals and their families

tourists (TOOR-ists) people who are traveling on vacation

wildlife reserves (WILDE-life ri-ZURVZ) protected areas where the killing of animals or the cutting down of trees is against the law

Index

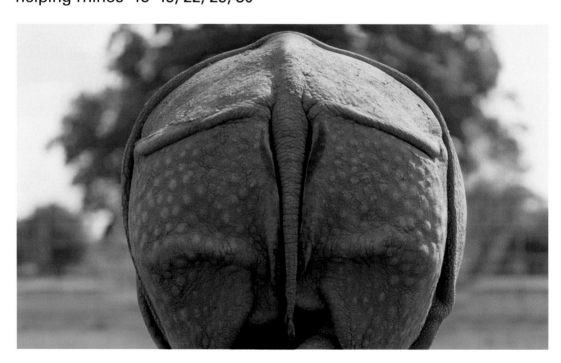